To our wonderful family,

and especially to John!

With special thanks to Maureen "Embee" Burns for the best clam chowder recipe ever
and to Penny Stratton for her wonderful editorial expertise.

Commonwealth Editions
An Imprint of Memoirs Unlimited, Inc.
21 Lothrop Street
Beverly, MA 01915
Visit us at www.commonwealtheditions.com.

ISBN 1-889833-40-1

10 9 8 7 6 5 4 3 2 1

Printed in Singapore

Journey Around Cape Cod & the Islands
cookbook

by Heather & Martha Zschock

COMMONWEALTH EDITIONS

Beverly, Massachusetts

contents

INTRODUCTION 7

THE WAMPANOAGS 8

Three Sisters Garden 10

Three Sisters Stew 11

Journey Pancakes 12

Corn Muffins 12

Maple Baked Beans 13

Succotash 13

Cornhusk Dolls 14

THE PILGRIMS 16

Anadama Bread 18

Boston Brown Bread 19

New England Boiled Dinner 20

Red Flannel Hash 20

Indian Pudding 21

Turkey Cutlets 22

Wild Rice 23

Baked Pear and Acorn Squash 23

Bayberry Candles 24

THE PORTUGUESE 26

Provincetown Kale Soup

(Caldo Verde) 28

Portuguese Sweet Bread

(Massa Cevada) 29

Portuguese Clam Chowder 30

Portuguese Flan 31

Sailor's Valentines 33

CRANBERRY HARVEST 34

Cranberry-Nut Muffins 36

Cranberry-Chocolate Nut Squares . . . 37

Cranberry Sauces 38

CATCH OF THE DAY 40

Marinades for Fish 42

Baked Haddock with

Garlic Breadcrumbs 44

Swordfish Kebabs 45

Sautéed Bass with Prosciutto 46

Salmon and Asparagus Risotto 47

Shellfish 48

  Clams and Lobsters 50

  Cocktail Sauce 51

  Clam Chowder 52

  Daddy's Stuffed Clams 53

  Clambake 54

  Stove-Top Clambake 55

  Steamed Mussels 56

  Linguini with Clam Sauce 57

  Fettucini with Scallops and Shrimp . . . 58

  Lobster Roll 59

Desserts 60

  Apple-Blueberry Pandowdy 62

  Yankee Doodle Shortcake 63

  Daffodil Cake 65

  A Cape Cod Legend 66

  S'mores 68

  Cranberry Fudge 69

  Penuche Fudge 69

  Drinks 70

Index 72

Greetings my friends,

and welcome to tasty Cape Cod and the Islands!

CAPE COD—SURROUNDED BY WATER, and dotted with freshwater ponds—is in a perfect geographical location for a bounty of fresh seafood. The area has a moderate climate—summer breezes off the water keep vacationers cool, while salty sea winds in the winter keep the temperature mild compared with the rest of New England. This hospitable climate contributes to the many delectable local ingredients.

Beach plums and cranberries flourish in the area's sandy and peaty soil, clams are available throughout the year, and fishing boats return with a fresh catch even on the coldest winter days.

Native Americans of the area fished, clammed, and hunted wild game. They relied on harvests of corn, as well as wild berries and nuts. Early settlers learned from the Native Americans and brought their own cooking methods, adapting them to local ingredients. Later, Portuguese settlers influenced many local dishes with their preference for simple, spicy food.

Although trends have varied over the years and more ingredients are available today, Cape Cod and the Islands maintain a unique flavor that is as distinct as the salty air on a summer morning. The most popular dishes are still some of the simplest, so grab your fishing poles and your clamming rakes, and let's start cooking!

The Wampanoags

Many traditional Cape Cod recipes are a combination of Native American and English ingredients. Long before the Pilgrims arrived, Cape Cod was inhabited by the Wampanoag Indians, or "eastern people." They were an agricultural tribe who supplemented their diets by hunting, fishing, and clamming. In the summer, they lived near the shore, in single-family dwellings called *wetus*, to take advantage of the bountiful supply

of fish and shellfish. During the colder months they moved into bark-covered communal "long houses," located inland where wild game was abundant.

Cornmeal, or "Indian meal," as the Pilgrims came to call it, was the diet staple of the Wampanoags and was eaten at almost every meal. Dried corn, preserved to last through the long winter months, was soaked in water and stir-fried to make hominy. Cornmeal mush was called hasty pudding, and eaten for breakfast or baked into pancakes called "johnny cakes," or "journey cakes." It was also made into hearty cornbread and corn pudding.

Wampanoag men were primarily responsible for hunting, fishing, trading, and clearing land for farming. To fish, they used stone spears and hooks made from bone, and they set up elaborate fishing weirs. Women gathered clams, nuts, and berries, and planted and tended to the gardens. The women also prepared, dried, and stored the food.

Cornmeal was made using wooden mortars and pestles.

Statue of Iyannough, Main Street Village Green, Hyannis

The Three Sisters

IN NATIVE AMERICAN TRADITION, corn, squash, and beans are the Three Sisters. When planted together, they support one another and flourish. This practice is based on the belief that all living things are intertwined and depend on each other to grow and survive. The corn stalks support the twining beans, the beans add nitrogen to the soil, and the squash planted at the base of the corn provides shade and keeps the ground moist.

Follow these steps for creating your own THREE SISTERS GARDEN:

1. Create a mound of dirt 1 foot high and 24 inches around. Plant 6 corn seeds in a circle in the center of the hill. Indians added fish (particularly herring, which was plentiful during the spring planting season) under the mound to add nutrients to the soil.

2. When the corn has sprouted, sow 6 squash seeds and 6 lima bean seeds around it.

3. As the plants grow, water your garden frequently, and make sure the corn stalks are supporting the beans.

THREE SISTERS STEW

INGREDIENTS

2 tablespoons olive oil
1 cup chopped onions
3 cloves garlic, chopped
1 tablespoon thyme
2 cups water
2 10-ounce cans concentrated chicken broth
¹/₂ cup white cooking wine
1¹/₂ cups frozen lima beans
1¹/₂ cups peeled and cubed butternut squash
1¹/₂ cups summer squash, halved vertically and sliced
1¹/₂ cups zucchini, halved vertically and sliced
1¹/₂ cups frozen corn
¹/₄ cup chopped fresh parsley
Salt and freshly ground pepper to taste

DIRECTIONS

Over medium heat, sauté the onion, garlic, and thyme in olive oil, stirring occasionally, until the onion becomes translucent. Add the water, chicken broth, white wine, and lima beans and bring to a boil. Boil for 5 minutes.

Add the remaining ingredients, return to a boil, and simmer, covered, on low heat for 15 to 20 minutes, or until the vegetables are tender.

Serves 6-8

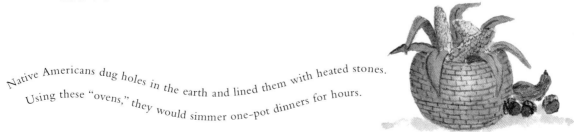

Native Americans dug holes in the earth and lined them with heated stones. Using these "ovens," they would simmer one-pot dinners for hours.

Journey Pancakes

The following recipe is a lighter variation of the traditional journey cakes—so called because travelers brought them on journeys to nibble along the way.

INGREDIENTS

$1^{1}/_{2}$ cups cornmeal
1 tablespoon sugar
$1^{1}/_{2}$ teaspoons salt
$1^{1}/_{2}$ cups boiling water
$^{1}/_{2}$ cup milk
$^{1}/_{2}$ cup finely chopped onions
$^{2}/_{3}$ cup chopped Canadian bacon
2 eggs, separated
2 teaspoons vegetable oil

DIRECTIONS

Mix together the cornmeal, sugar, salt, and boiling water in a large bowl. Set aside for 5 to 10 minutes. Mix in the milk, chopped onions, Canadian bacon, and egg yolks.

In a separate bowl, beat the egg whites until they are light and fluffy. Mix half the egg whites into the cornmeal batter, then fold in the remaining half. Heat the oil in a large frying pan over medium heat. Pour in spoonfuls of the batter. Cook approximately 2 to 3 minutes per side.

Serves 4

Corn Muffins

INGREDIENTS

$^{3}/_{4}$ cup cornmeal
$1^{1}/_{4}$ cups flour
$^{1}/_{4}$ cup sugar
2 teaspoons baking powder
$^{1}/_{2}$ teaspoon salt
1 egg
$^{1}/_{4}$ cup melted butter
1 cup milk

DIRECTIONS

Preheat the oven to 400°. Lightly grease a 12-cup muffin pan or line it with paper muffin liners.

In a large bowl, whisk together the cornmeal, flour, sugar, baking powder, and salt. In a separate bowl, whisk together the egg, melted butter, and milk. Add the wet ingredients to the dry ingredients and stir just enough to moisten them. Spoon the batter into prepared muffin cups.

Bake for 15 to 20 minutes, or until a toothpick inserted into a muffin comes out clean. Set aside until cool to prevent the muffins from sticking to the muffin papers.

Makes 12 muffins

Journey cakes are also called "hoe cakes," because they were occasionally cooked in an open fire on a hoe!

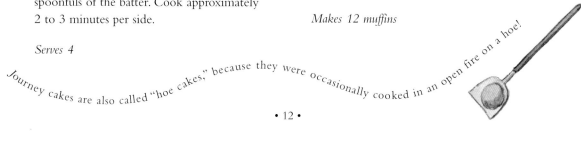

MAPLE BAKED BEANS

INGREDIENTS

2 cups dried navy beans, rinsed
8 cups water
2 teaspoons salt
1 large garlic clove, chopped
¹/₄ cup maple syrup
¹/₂ cup light molasses
1 ¹/₂ teaspoons dry mustard
¹/₄ pound salt pork
1 onion, quartered

DIRECTIONS

In a large ovenproof kettle, combine the beans with the water and 1 teaspoon salt, and bring to a boil. Simmer, covered, over medium heat for 1¹/₂ hours.

Preheat the oven to 325°. Drain the beans, and save the liquid. Return the beans to the kettle.

In a bowl, combine the chopped garlic, maple syrup, molasses, mustard, and remaining salt. Pour the mixture over the beans, and add just enough of the reserved cooking liquid to cover the beans. Score the salt pork and poke it into the middle of the beans along with the quartered onion.

Bake the beans, covered, for 3 hours. Check every 45 minutes, adding just enough water to keep the mixture covered.

Serves 6

SUCCOTASH

INGREDIENTS

2 tablespoons olive oil
1 onion, chopped
2 cups frozen baby lima beans
2 cups frozen corn
6 strips cooked bacon, chopped
1 teaspoon sugar
¹/₄ cup heavy cream
2 tablespoons chopped fresh parsley
Salt and pepper to taste

DIRECTIONS

In a small saucepan, sauté the chopped onions in olive oil until they become translucent. Set aside.

Bring the water to a boil in a medium pot. Add the frozen lima beans to the boiling water and cook them for 10 minutes. Add the frozen corn, and cook for 5 more minutes. Drain the vegetables and return them to the pot. Add the onions, bacon, sugar, heavy cream, parsley, and salt and pepper to taste. Simmer over low heat for 10 minutes.

Serves 4

cornhusk dolls

NATIVE AMERICANS USED ALL PARTS OF THE CORN PLANT—nothing was wasted. Corncobs were burned for fuel, and cornhusks were woven into useful domestic items such as baskets and sleeping mats. Children made dolls from the cornhusks, and they used cornsilk for the dolls' hair. Yellow, early-season silk made blond hair, and mid- to late-season silk made brown hair.

Follow these steps to create your own CORNHUSK DOLL:

MATERIALS

*10-12 pieces of fresh or dried corn husks (if using dried husks,
    soak them in water until they are soft and pliable)*
String
Scissors
Beads, paint, shells, and colored yarn or ribbon

Group 4 cornhusks together.

Tie them tightly together 1 inch from the top.

Pull the longer ends of the husks down as shown.

Tie the husks together with string to form the "head."

To create the doll's arms, take 1 husk and roll it into a tube. Tie each end with string and insert it between the husks, under the "neck."

Tie the string tightly under the arms to form the doll's body.

Arrange four more husks around the doll's waist, and tie tightly to form a skirt.

Place two more husks diagonally over the shoulders and tie at the waist with a string. Trim the ends to create the desired skirt length.

For the final touch, add pretty faces and snazzy hairdos, and decorate your doll with beads, paint, shells, and colored yarn or ribbon.

The Pilgrims

When the first settlers arrived on the *Mayflower*, they were not prepared to survive the harsh winter months. Fortunately for them, the Wampanoag Indians they met were friendly and helpful. They gave the Pilgrims food and taught them how to farm, hunt, and fish. They introduced them to new ingredients, such as corn, maple syrup, cranberries, shellfish, and long-storing root vegetables. The Pilgrims adapted these new ingredients to their own cooking methods. This fusion of Native American and English cooking is the basis of many recipes that are still popular on Cape Cod today.

The Pilgrims learned how to grow and prepare corn, and it became a staple part of their diets. Some of the animals they hunted for food were deer, turkeys, rabbits, geese, and pheasant. The shores of Cape Cod provided a bountiful supply of seafood and shellfish, especially clams, oysters, lobster, and cod.

A common meal, which combined Pilgrim frugality and simplicity, was the robust New England boiled dinner, a one-pot stew of meat and vegetables that simmered all day. Another popular one-pot meal was chowder, a seafood stew consisting of clams and/or fish in a thick, creamy soup, flavored with salt pork and diced potatoes.

The land provided an abundance of native fruits, including many types of berries. The Pilgrims used them to make a variety of puddings and pies, hearty desserts that were often combined with cornmeal, maple syrup, or molasses.

Provincetown Harbor

ANADAMA BREAD

Anadama bread is a New England specialty made with cornmeal and molasses. There is much speculation over the name of this bread. According to one legend, the proud husband of a great bread maker named Anna exclaims, "Anna, damn her!" every time he eats a slice of her delicious bread.

INGREDIENTS

$^1/_2$ cup water
$^1/_3$ cup cornmeal
2 tablespoons butter, softened
$^1/_2$ cup light molasses
1 package active dry yeast

$^1/_2$–$^3/_4$ cup warm water
2 cups bread flour
1 cup whole wheat flour
1 teaspoon salt

DIRECTIONS

In a small saucepan, bring $^1/_2$ cup water and the cornmeal to a boil over medium heat, stirring occasionally. Cook and continue stirring for about 5 minutes until the mixture thickens. Remove from the heat and stir in the butter and molasses. Set aside and let cool to lukewarm.

Dissolve the yeast in $^1/_2$ cup warm water and set aside for 10 minutes as the cornmeal mixture cools. The yeast mixture will appear somewhat foamy and creamy as it "blooms."

In a large bowl, combine the yeast and cornmeal mixtures until they are well blended. Sift the bread flour, whole wheat flour, and salt in a separate bowl, and add to the yeast mixture 1 cup at a time, stirring well. Add an additional $^1/_4$ cup warm water if needed to form a soft, not sticky, dough. Turn out onto a lightly floured surface and knead for 10 minutes.

Lightly oil a large mixing bowl. Add the dough, and then flip it upside down so that the entire surface is lightly oiled. Cover the bowl with a damp cloth and place it in a warm, draft-free spot to rise for 1 to 1$^1/_2$ hours, until the dough has doubled in size.

Punch down the dough, and turn it out onto a lightly floured surface. Place it in a lightly greased 9 x 5-inch loaf pan, and cover it with a damp cloth. Place it in a warm spot for approximately 45 minutes, or until the dough has doubled in size.

Bake at 375° for 25 to 30 minutes, or until the top is a deep golden brown. Tap the bottom of the loaf pan. If it sounds hollow, the bread is done.

Makes 1 loaf

BOSTON BROWN BREAD

INGREDIENTS

1 cup brown bread flour, or equal parts whole wheat flour, rye flour, and cornmeal
³/₄ teaspoon baking soda
¹/₂ teaspoon salt
³/₄ cup buttermilk
¹/₄ cup dark molasses
¹/₂ cup dried cranberries
10-ounce coffee can

DIRECTIONS

Whisk together the flour, baking soda, and salt in a large mixing bowl. Stir in the buttermilk and molasses and mix well. Fold in the dried cranberries. Generously butter the coffee can and spoon in the batter.

Cover the top of the coffee can with a double layer of aluminum foil. Pinch the sides down securely so the foil cover is airtight and secure.

Place the coffee can in a large kettle and add boiling water so that the water comes halfway up the sides of the can. Cover the kettle and steam for approximately 1½ hours until the bread rises and a wooden skewer inserted in the center comes out clean.

Remove the can from the kettle and allow it to cool. Open the reverse end with a can opener. Push the bread out through the bottom. Let it cool for a few minutes to prevent crumbling before slicing. Cut thick round slices to serve.

Makes 1 loaf

Kettles hung on chains in the hearths. The chains could be raised or lowered to achieve the desired cooking temperature.

New England Boiled Dinner

INGREDIENTS

4 pounds corned beef roast
2 bay leaves
3 cloves garlic, peeled
3 whole cloves
8 small or 4 medium fresh beets
2 large onions, peeled and halved

4 small turnips, peeled and halved
7 carrots, scraped and cut into large chunks
6 medium red potatoes, halved
1 medium head of cabbage, cut in wedges
¼ cup chopped fresh parsley
Salt and pepper to taste

DIRECTIONS

Rinse the roast in cold water. Place it in a large kettle, cover it with cold water, and bring it to a boil. Skim off any foam that rises to the top during the first 5 minutes of cooking. Add the bay leaves, garlic, and cloves. Reduce the heat to low, and simmer, covered, for about 2½ hours.

In a separate pot, cook the beets in boiling water for 30 minutes, until tender. Drain and peel them, then set them aside and keep them warm.

After the meat has cooked for 2 hours, add the onions, turnips, carrots, potatoes, and cabbage to the pot. Continue cooking for 30 minutes.

Remove the roast and carve it into thin slices. Serve it on a platter surrounded by the vegetables. Sprinkle with fresh parsley and salt and pepper to taste. Serve with mustard or horseradish.

Serves 6

Red Flannel Hash

New Englanders are never ones to waste food. Red flannel hash, named after the color of long johns, was traditionally made from the leftovers of a New England boiled dinner. Preheat oven to 400°. Toss last night's leftovers together in a dish and roughly chop. Heat 2 tablespoons butter in an ovenproof skillet and add leftovers. Pat down and cook over low heat until hash begins to brown at the edges, about 15 minutes. Place skillet in oven for about 15 minutes, until the top begins to brown.

INDIAN PUDDING

Native Americans didn't actually make this pudding since they didn't cook with milk or eggs. It is called "Indian pudding" because it was made with corn, and the colonists had a tendency to refer to any food made with corn as "Indian."

INGREDIENTS

1 cup milk
4 cups half and half
³/₄ cup cornmeal
¹/₄ cup sugar
¹/₄ cup brown sugar
¹/₂ cup light molasses

1 teaspoon salt
1 tablespoon butter
1 teaspoon cinnamon
¹/₄ teaspoon ginger
¹/₂ cup dried cranberries
Vanilla ice cream

DIRECTIONS

Preheat the oven to 325°. Grease a 9 x 5 x 3-inch glass loaf pan.

Combine the milk, 1 cup of half and half, and cornmeal in a medium saucepan. Cook over medium heat, whisking frequently, until the mixture comes to a boil. Reduce the heat to low, and continue stirring until the mixture thickens and becomes creamy.

Add the sugar, brown sugar, molasses, salt, butter, cinnamon, ginger, dried cranberries, and 2 cups of half and half (saving the last cup until later). Stir to combine. Bring the mixture back to a boil. The mixture will thicken as it begins to boil. When it does, transfer it to the prepared loaf pan.

Fill a larger pan halfway with boiling water. Place the loaf pan inside the larger pan. Bake for 1 hour, stirring occasionally.

Stir in the remaining cup of half and half after the pudding has baked for 1 hour. Bake for 1 more hour, stirring occasionally. Serve while still warm with vanilla ice cream.

Serves 6

TURKEY CUTLETS

The first "Thanksgiving" was actually a traditional English harvest celebration. In 1621, with help from the Wampanoags, the Pilgrims had a bountiful harvest and food that could be stored away for the winter months. To express their gratitude, they invited their Native American neighbors to a celebratory feast, which lasted for three days.

INGREDIENTS

2 pounds turkey cutlets
1 cup orange juice
$1/2$ teaspoon ground sage
$1/2$ teaspoon rosemary
$1/4$ teaspoon salt
$1/4$ teaspoon pepper
1 cup raspberries
1 teaspoon sugar
Orange slices, halved

DIRECTIONS

Preheat the oven to 400°. Rinse the turkey cutlets and place them in a baking dish large enough to accommodate a single layer.

Mix the orange juice, ground sage, rosemary, salt, and pepper in a bowl, and pour over the turkey cutlets. Marinate for $1/2$ hour.

In a small bowl, gently mash the raspberries and sugar together, and spoon the mixture over the cutlets. Bake for 15 to 20 minutes. Garnish with orange slices.

Serves 4

President Lincoln proclaimed the first national Thanksgiving Day holiday in 1863.

WILD RICE

INGREDIENTS

7 ounces long-grain wild rice
2 ¼ cups water
2 chicken bouillon cubes
2 tablespoons butter

1 medium onion, chopped
1 tablespoon olive oil
2 tablespoons fresh parsley

DIRECTIONS

Combine the rice, water, bouillon cubes, and butter in a medium saucepan and bring to a boil. Reduce the heat to medium and simmer for 25 to 30 minutes.

Sauté the onions in olive oil until they become translucent. Mix them, along with the parsley, into the wild rice a few minutes before it has finished cooking.

Serves 4

BAKED PEAR AND ACORN SQUASH

INGREDIENTS

2 acorn squash, split in half and seeded
1 cup chopped pear
¼ cup orange juice

3 tablespoons brown sugar
4 teaspoons butter

DIRECTIONS

Preheat the oven to 400°. Place the squash, cut side up, in a baking dish. Add 1 inch of water to the dish.

In a small bowl, combine the pear, orange juice, and brown sugar. Put 1 teaspoon of butter in each squash half, and fill with the pear mixture. Bake for 45 minutes to 1 hour, until the squash is soft.

Serves 4

Bayberry Candles

EARLY WOMEN SETTLERS OF CAPE COD discovered that when they warmed bayberries in water, the berries released an aromatic wax that floated to the surface. In late fall, they would pick buckets of the berries from evergreen bushes to make candles. They rinsed the berries and heated them in water-filled kettles. Once the wax floated to the surface, the women would dip wicks—attached to rods made of cattails—into the kettles to form the candles. It takes about 5 to 8 pounds of berries to make 1 pound of wax, so it is time-consuming work. As a result, bayberry wax is one of the most expensive types of wax to buy today.

Cape Cod legend has it
that a bayberry candle burned
down to the socket on New Year's
Eve will bring health to the home
and wealth to the pocket.

HOW TO MAKE YOUR OWN BAYBERRY CANDLES...

...without picking 12 pounds of bayberries

Purchase materials from a craft store or from an Internet source. These instructions are for a simple dipping method that early settlers would have used, but you can also use candle molds or other methods.

MATERIALS

2 pounds premium taper wax
Bayberry scent
Sage coloring

Tall metal container
Candle wicking
Cattail rods (or a pencil!) to tie wicks to

DIRECTIONS

Place 1½ to 2 pounds of wax into the metal container. Add the desired amount of scent and coloring (usually one square per pound of wax). Put the container in a large pot partially filled with water. Heat the wax to 160° over medium heat.

Tie 2 pieces of 10-inch wicking to a cattail rod (or pencil) about 2 inches apart. Dip the wicks into the wax, remove them quickly, and allow them to cool slightly. Straighten the wick with your fingers.

Continue dipping the wicks into the container, allowing the wax to cool between each dip. If the wax is too hot, it will not adhere well to the wick, and the wax on the wick may melt. Once the candles reach a desired thickness, set them aside, and continue to make as many candles as you like. To create a smooth finish, heat the wax to 180° and dip the candles in for 3 seconds. This will slightly melt the outer layer. You might need to cut the base of the candles to fit them into candleholders.

The Portuguese

During the peak of the whaling industry, in the early 1800s, captains recruited Portuguese seamen for their whaling vessels. Most of them came from the Azores or the Cape Verde Islands—both ports of call along whaling routes. Hard workers, they were eager for economic opportunities in

America. As the whaling industry began to decline during the latter part of the 1800s, many Portuguese settled in Provincetown, on the tip of Cape Cod, and became fishermen. They brought over their families from Portugal as soon as they were able, forming a close-knit community.

The Portuguese like spicy food, and not surprisingly many of their recipes call for fish. Spices and marinades such as *vinho d'alhos* added flavor, and helped preserve food, especially in the days before refrigeration. Popular dishes incorporated salt pork, cod fish, and the Portuguese sausages, *linguiça* and *chourico*.

Kale soup, or *caldo verde* (or *couves*, Portuguese for "cabbage"), has always been a Portuguese favorite in Provincetown. Containing vegetables, potatoes, and meat or sausage, it is highly nutritious and inexpensive to make. Kale, a member of the cabbage family, is a hardy vegetable that is easy to grow in the Cape Cod climate.

When a captain returned from a long voyage, his family would place a pineapple outside the house to let friends know they were welcome to hear of his adventures.

Blessing of the Fleet, Provincetown

PROVINCETOWN KALE SOUP (*Caldo Verde*)

There is much debate in Provincetown over the best way to make this hearty soup…with linguiça or pork, with tomatoes, or without? The recipes tend to vary as much as the cooks themselves! This basic recipe may inspire you to create your own family recipe.

INGREDIENTS

2 tablespoons olive oil
³/₄ pound linguiça, sliced, with casing removed
3 medium Yukon Gold potatoes, peeled and diced
1 cup chopped onions
1 quart chicken broth
1 pound kale, coarsely chopped
2 tablespoons chopped garlic
1 15-ounce can kidney beans, drained and rinsed
1 tablespoon vinegar
2 teaspoons salt
Ground pepper to taste

DIRECTIONS

Heat the oil in a deep kettle over medium high heat. Sauté the *linguiça*, potatoes, and onions for 5 minutes, stirring occasionally.

Add 2 cups of the chicken broth, the kale, and the garlic and simmer for 3 to 5 minutes, until the kale wilts. Add the remaining chicken broth, along with the beans, vinegar, salt, and pepper, and bring to a boil. Reduce the heat to medium and simmer for 30 minutes.

Serves 6

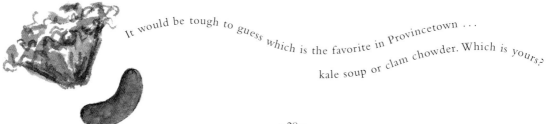

It would be tough to guess which is the favorite in Provincetown … kale soup or clam chowder. Which is yours?

PORTUGUESE SWEET BREAD (*Massa Cevada*)

INGREDIENTS

1 package active dry yeast
¼ cup very hot water
½ cup milk
¼ cup butter

2 eggs
½ cup sugar
½ teaspoon salt
3–3½ cups flour

DIRECTIONS

Dissolve the yeast in the hot water and set it aside for 10 minutes. The yeast mixture will appear somewhat foamy and creamy as it "blooms."

In a small saucepan, heat the milk and butter over low heat until the butter melts.

Whisk the milk mixture together with the eggs, sugar, and salt. Stir in the yeast mixture and gradually add the flour until the dough holds together in a ball. The dough will be quite sticky, so coat your hands with flour, and knead the dough on a lightly floured surface for 10 minutes. The dough should be smooth, soft, and elastic.

Lightly oil a large mixing bowl. Add the dough, and then flip it upside down so that the entire surface is lightly oiled. Cover the bowl with a warm, wet cloth and place it in a warm, draft-free spot. Allow the dough to rise for 1½ hours, until it has doubled.

Punch down the dough and knead it on a lightly floured surface for 3 minutes. Grease a pie pan, form the dough into a ball, and place it in the center of the pan. Cover with a warm, damp cloth and allow the dough to rise until doubled in size, about 1½ hours.

Preheat the oven to 350°. Bake the bread for 30 minutes, until the crust is golden brown and a skewer inserted into the center comes out clean.

Makes 1 loaf

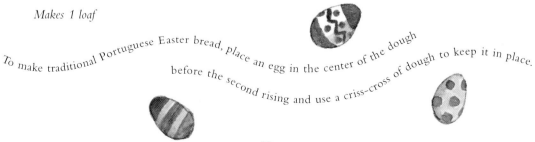

To make traditional Portuguese Easter bread, place an egg in the center of the dough before the second rising and use a criss-cross of dough to keep it in place.

PORTUGUESE CLAM CHOWDER

This recipe calls for scallops and Little Neck clams. The Portuguese settlers used what was available depending on the seasons. Other types of seafood—mussels, lobster, and haddock, or other firm white fish—would also work well in this simple recipe.

INGREDIENTS

2 tablespoons olive oil
4 ounces linguiça, chopped
6 ounces Canadian bacon, chopped
1 cup chopped onions
1 cup diced celery
2 cups chopped tomatoes
3 cloves garlic, chopped
Salt and pepper to taste

3 baking potatoes, diced
2 cups chicken broth
4 cups white wine
1 tablespoon vinegar
1 cup Little Neck clams, chopped
1 cup bay scallops
1/2 cup finely chopped parsley

DIRECTIONS

Heat the olive oil in a large kettle over medium heat. Add the *linguiça*, Canadian bacon, onions, and celery, and sauté for 5 minutes. Add the tomatoes and garlic and continue to sauté for 2 minutes. Season with salt and pepper. Stir in the potatoes, chicken stock, white wine, and vinegar.

Bring the chowder to a boil, reduce the heat, and simmer for 20 minutes. Add the clams, scallops, and parsley. Cover, and continue simmering for 5 minutes.

Serves 6

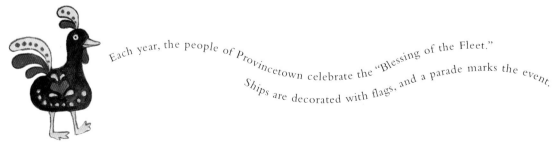

Each year, the people of Provincetown celebrate the "Blessing of the Fleet." Ships are decorated with flags, and a parade marks the event.

PORTUGUESE FLAN

INGREDIENTS

1 ²/₃ cups sugar
3 whole eggs
3 egg yolks

3 cups half and half
2 teaspoons vanilla
¹/₄ teaspoon cinnamon

DIRECTIONS

Preheat the oven to 350°. In a medium saucepan, cook 1 cup sugar over medium heat, stirring frequently until it is dark golden brown, thickens, and begins to smell like caramel, about 5 to 10 minutes. Carefully pour the mixture into a 9-inch round baking dish, and swirl it over the bottom and sides to coat. Set aside.

Gently whisk together the eggs and egg yolks, trying not to whisk in any air. Gradually add the half and half, vanilla, remaining ²/₃ cup sugar, and cinnamon. Pour over the caramel in the baking dish. Place the dish in a larger baking dish. Add enough hot water to come halfway up the sides of the inner dish.

Bake for approximately 45 minutes, until a knife inserted near the center comes out clean. The center should remain somewhat jiggly because it will continue to cook once the dish is removed from the oven. Allow it to cool in the water bath, and then refrigerate the flan for an hour before serving.

To unmold the flan, run a sharp knife around the sides of the dish. Place the bottom of the dish in a pan of very hot tap water, removing after a few seconds. Place a serving platter over the top of the baking dish, and invert both quickly.

Serves 8-10

During the 1940s, Peter Hunt established a workshop in Provincetown called Peter Hunt's Peasant Village. Using bold brushstrokes, he painted folk designs on second-hand furniture, which became wildly popular.

Sailor's Valentines

SAILOR'S VALENTINES, intricately detailed mosaics created with shells, were popular gifts from sailors to their sweethearts during the Victorian era. Traditional sailor's valentines featured floral designs, hearts, and sentimental messages. They were usually inset in two-sided, hinged wooden boxes.

Historians debate whether these valentines were first created by sailors with time to spare or by skilled craftsmen. Research indicates that they were

made on the island of Barbados, a frequent stop for seafaring vessels. Of the thirty-five kinds of shells that were typically used in a sailor's valentine, all are local to Barbados. Also, the intricate work involved, and the length of time the glue would need to dry, would make construction very difficult on a rocking ship.

The shores of the Cape offer a wide assortment of shells that might inspire you to create your own sailor's valentine. Find or purchase a plain wooden box with a lid. Using clear-drying glue, coat the bottom of the inside of the box. Lay a pattern of shells inside the box. Add personal notes, photos, beads, or postcards to create a lovely souvenir of your trip to the Cape!

People of the Victorian era were avid collectors, and they loved the boxes for their variety of shell specimens.

Cranberry Harvest

Cranberries have played an important role in the history of Cape Cod. Long ago, sailors brought barrels of nutritious cranberries with them on voyages. Rich in vitamin C, cranberries helped prevent a disease called scurvy.

Native Americans of the area called cranberries *ibimi*, or "bitterberry." They sweetened them with maple sugar and ate them raw, or mixed them into other dishes. The berries also served as a medicinal ingredient to draw poison from arrow wounds, and as a natural red dye for fabrics.

Cranberries grow on vines in moist, sandy areas called bogs. Each autumn, growers harvest cranberries using two different methods—wet and dry harvesting. Cranberries destined for the fresh fruit market are dry-harvested with a mechanical picker, which combs the vines and deposits the berries into containers. Berries are carefully sorted, and only those that remain intact will be sent to the markets. Before this technology, workers harvested the berries using a cranberry scoop. School was suspended during the harvest, and everyone was expected to help.

Cranberries that will be used for juices and sauces are wet-harvested. The bogs are flooded the night before the harvest. The following day, a machine known as an "egg beater" churns the water, causing the berries to loosen from the vines and rise to the surface. The berries are corralled into a beautiful sea of red and are pumped from the bogs.

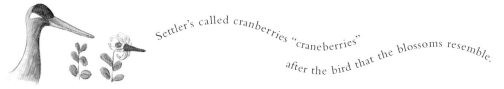

Settler's called cranberries "craneberries" after the bird that the blossoms resemble.

Cranberry Bog, Harwich

CRANBERRY-NUT MUFFINS

INGREDIENTS

1 cup dried cranberries
3 teaspoons grated orange peel
1 cup buttermilk
1 stick unsalted butter, at room temperature
$^3/_4$ cup sugar
2 eggs, lightly beaten
1 $^3/_4$ cups flour
1 teaspoon baking soda
2 teaspoons baking powder
$^1/_2$ cup chopped walnuts (optional)
Pinch of salt

DIRECTIONS

Combine the dried cranberries, orange peel, and buttermilk in a small bowl and let the mixture sit for 30 minutes. Preheat the oven to 350°. Lightly grease a 12-cup muffin pan or line it with paper muffin liners.

Cream the butter and sugar in a large bowl. Add the eggs and mix thoroughly. Sift in the flour, baking soda, baking powder, walnuts, and salt. Stir the cranberry mixture into the batter.

Fill the muffin tins three-quarters full. Bake for 15 to 20 minutes, until a toothpick inserted in the center comes out clean. Allow the muffins to cool on a wire rack before serving.

Makes 12 muffins

Cranberries are judged by their color, size, firmness, and bounce. The fresher a cranberry is, the higher it bounces!

CRANBERRY-CHOCOLATE NUT SQUARES

Native Americans used cranberries to make pemmican, a mixture of deer meat, cranberries, and fat—this country's first energy bar! They brought it on long journeys and hunting expeditions because it lasted a long time without spoiling. The combination seems distasteful today, so we suggest this treat instead for a long day at the beach or an afternoon tea.

INGREDIENTS

Base:

1 cup flour
$^1/_2$ cup butter, at room temperature
3 tablespoons confectioner's sugar

Topping:

2 eggs
1 cup sugar
$^1/_4$ cup flour
$^1/_2$ teaspoon baking powder
$^1/_4$ teaspoon salt

1 teaspoon vanilla
$^3/_4$ cup chopped walnuts
$^1/_2$ cup coconut
$^1/_2$ cup dried cranberries
$^1/_2$ cup semisweet chocolate chips

DIRECTIONS

Base:

Preheat the oven to 350° and grease an 8 x 8-inch baking pan. Beat the flour, butter, and confectioner's sugar in a small bowl until smooth. Spread the mixture in a thin, even layer in the baking pan. Bake 20 to 25 minutes until lightly browned.

Topping:

Beat the eggs together in a medium bowl. Stir in the remaining ingredients. Spread evenly over the top of the cooked base, and bake for 25 minutes. Cool before serving.

Makes 8 squares

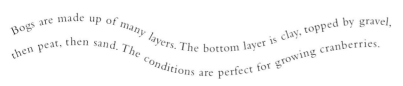

Bogs are made up of many layers. The bottom layer is clay, topped by gravel, then peat, then sand. The conditions are perfect for growing cranberries.

cranberry sauces

CRAN-RASPBERRY VINAIGRETTE

INGREDIENTS

2 tablespoons balsamic vinegar
2 tablespoons lemon juice
¼ teaspoon brown sugar
2 teaspoons honey
1 teaspoon chopped parsley
¼ cup olive oil
¼ cup chopped frozen cranberries, thawed
¼ cup raspberries
Salt and pepper to taste

DIRECTIONS

Combine the balsamic vinegar, lemon juice, brown sugar, honey, and parsley. Slowly whisk in the olive oil. Stir in the chopped cranberries and raspberries. Add salt and pepper to taste.

Serves 4

CRANBERRY-APPLE-PEAR SAUCE

INGREDIENTS

6 large apples, peeled and quartered
4 large pears, peeled and quartered
2 cups chopped frozen cranberries
1 cup sugar
1 teaspoon cinnamon
3 strips lemon zest
¼ cup water
1 teaspoon vanilla
¼ teaspoon ground nutmeg

DIRECTIONS

Place the apples and pears in a medium saucepan. Add the cranberries, sugar, cinnamon, and lemon zest. Add the water and bring to a boil. Cover and simmer over medium heat until the fruit is tender.

Remove from the heat, and stir in the vanilla and nutmeg. Let stand for 30 minutes, discard the lemon zest, and stir before serving.

Serves 6

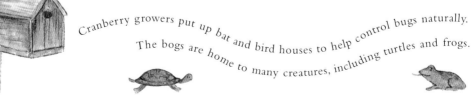

Cranberry growers put up bat and bird houses to help control bugs naturally. The bogs are home to many creatures, including turtles and frogs.

CRANBERRY SAUCE

INGREDIENTS

2 cups frozen cranberries, thawed and drained
1 cup sugar
1 1/2 teaspoons lemon juice
3/4 cup orange juice
1/2 teaspoon grated lemon peel
1/4 teaspoon cinnamon

DIRECTIONS

In medium saucepan over medium heat, combine the cranberries, sugar, lemon juice, and orange juice. Bring to a boil, stirring frequently. Stir in the lemon peel and cinnamon. Reduce the heat to low, cover, and simmer for 10 minutes. Chill until ready to serve.

Serves 4

CRANBERRY-PEAR CHUTNEY

INGREDIENTS

2 cups cranberries
1 cup sugar
2 oranges, peeled and cut in chunks
1/4 cup raisins
1 pear, peeled, cored, and chopped
1/2 teaspoon white vinegar
1/4 teaspoon cinnamon
1/4 teaspoon ground ginger

DIRECTIONS

Combine all the ingredients in a large saucepan and simmer over medium heat for 20 minutes. Remove from heat and stir with a masher. Refrigerate before serving.

Serves 4

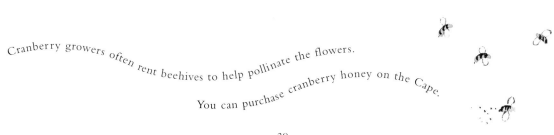

Cranberry growers often rent beehives to help pollinate the flowers. You can purchase cranberry honey on the Cape.

Catch of the Day

Cape Cod…the name says it all! An abundance of fresh fish are caught daily in the waters all along the sandy shores and in over 360 freshwater ponds dotting the Cape. Geographically, the Cape is a perfect place to fish. It lies to the west of the fertile fishing grounds of Stellwagen Bank, and it is positioned along a migratory route for fish following the Gulf Stream as it flows northward.

Historically, many Cape Codders have prospered from careers at sea. Many beautiful historic homes on the Cape and Islands once belonged to wealthy fishing or whaling captains. Commercial fishing continues to be a thriving industry on the Cape, although there are now many restrictions to contend with. Recreational fishing is, as always, a popular sport that lures many hopefuls to the Cape each year.

Anyone can catch bluefish and bass by surfcasting from the sandy beaches or dropping a line off one of the many jetties and piers lining the Cape and Islands (look for a flock of seagulls offshore, and you'll know a school of bluefish is nearby!). Or, if you're up for a day of adventure, many local fishing boats offer day trips farther offshore. Those who arrive at the fish piers when the boats come in have been known to receive a fresh fish or two! There are many ways to prepare the local fish. The following recipes offer a variety of cooking methods, which will bring out the wonderful flavor of fresh fish.

Rock Harbor, Orleans

marinades *for fish*

COOKING TIPS

FISH USUALLY COOKS VERY QUICKLY. *You'll know it's fully cooked when the flesh looks white or opaque (no longer slightly translucent), and when you can easily insert a fork or skewer into it.*

As a general guideline, cook fish for 5 to 10 minutes per inch of thickness, although this time might vary depending on the intensity of the heat and the method of cooking: baking, broiling, grilling, poaching, steaming, or sautéing.

Fish has a tendency to dry out very quickly. Marinades can add moisture to the fish while enhancing the flavor. Marinades are usually created with a fatty ingredient such as oil or butter; an acidic ingredient, such as wine or citrus; and flavoring spices. Refrigerate fish during marination.

Mix up some of these suggestions, or have fun creating your own!

GARLIC-DILL MARINADE

INGREDIENTS

1 cup olive oil
1/4 cup fresh lemon juice
3 cloves garlic, chopped
Fresh dill, chopped
Salt and pepper to taste

ORANGE-BASIL MARINADE

INGREDIENTS

1/2 cup olive oil
1/4 cup chopped basil leaves
1 teaspoon grated orange peel
1 clove garlic, chopped
1/4 cup fresh orange juice
Salt and pepper to taste

WHITE WINE MARINADE

INGREDIENTS

2 cups light white wine
2 tablespoons lemon juice
2 tablespoons Dijon mustard
¼ cup chopped fresh parsley
Salt and pepper to taste

ASIAN STYLE MARINADE

INGREDIENTS

1 cup soy sauce
¼ cup sesame oil
¼ cup rice vinegar
2 tablespoons honey
3 cloves garlic, chopped
1 tablespoon minced ginger
1 scallion, thinly sliced
Salt and pepper to taste

VINHO D'ALHOS

INGREDIENTS

1 cup white wine vinegar
3 cups water
3 cloves garlic, chopped
½ teaspoon cumin
½ teaspoon black pepper
½ teaspoon salt

ROSEMARY-THYME MARINADE

INGREDIENTS

1 cup dry white wine
½ cup orange juice
½ cup fresh lemon juice
3 tablespoons soy sauce
½ cup chopped red onions
3 cloves garlic, chopped
1 tablespoon rosemary
1 tablespoon thyme
2 tablespoons chopped fresh parsley
Salt and pepper to taste

There are no licenses required for saltwater fishing on the Cape, although there are certain restrictions. Check at a local bait and tackle store to get the lowdown. You *will* need to purchase a license from the town offices to fish in freshwater ponds and lakes.

INGREDIENTS

2 pounds haddock fillets
¹/₂ cup white cooking wine
Juice of 1 lemon
¹/₄ teaspoon salt
¹/₄ teaspoon ground black pepper
²/₃ cup butter
4 cloves garlic, chopped
1 cup bread crumbs
¹/₄ cup chopped fresh parsley
8 thinly sliced lemon rounds

DIRECTIONS

Preheat the oven to 375°. In a baking dish large enough to hold the fish fillets in a single layer, marinate the fish in the cooking wine, lemon juice, salt, and pepper for 15 minutes per side.

In a small saucepan, melt the butter, then add the chopped garlic and sauté on low heat for 1 minute. Stir in the bread crumbs and parsley. Spoon an equal amount of the bread crumb mixture onto the top of each fillet.

Bake for approximately 10 to 15 minutes, depending on the thickness of the fish. The fish should be flaky and the bread-crumbs golden brown. Place 2 lemon rounds on the top of each fillet for garnish.

Serves 4

Local fleets unload their catch every day at the Chatham Fish Pier. The Provider, overlooking the pier, is dedicated to fisherfolk.

SWORDFISH KEBABS

1 ¼ pounds swordfish
7 ounces prepared pesto
½ cup light white wine
1 tablespoon Dijon mustard
Juice of ½ lemon
8 ounces medium mushrooms
1 zucchini
1 summer squash
1–2 red peppers
1 large onion
2 tablespoons olive oil
Salt and pepper to taste

DIRECTIONS

Cut the swordfish into 1-inch chunks. Combine the pesto, wine, mustard, and lemon juice. Add the swordfish to the mixture and marinate for 1 to 4 hours in the refrigerator.

Cut the zucchini, summer squash, peppers, and onion into 1-inch pieces. Toss the vegetables with the olive oil, salt, and pepper. Spear the swordfish and vegetables onto skewers and grill or broil for 4 minutes per side.

Serves 4

Before refrigeration, salt was used to preserve food. Captain John Sears invented a way to evaporate water from seawater, leaving the salt behind.

INGREDIENTS

1³/₄–2 pounds bass fillet
Pepper
Garlic salt
2 tablespoons coarsely chopped fresh sage
3 tablespoons olive oil
8 slices prosciutto
¹/₃ cup white wine
1 tablespoon Dijon mustard
1 tablespoon butter

DIRECTIONS

Skin the bass fillet if necessary, and divide it into 4 equal pieces. Sprinkle the fillets with pepper, garlic salt and sage. Wrap each fillet with 2 slices of prosciutto.

Heat the olive oil on medium heat in a saucepan large enough to hold all the fillets. Sauté the fillet bundles on each side until they are lightly browned. Add the white wine, mustard, and butter.

Reduce the heat to simmer, cover the saucepan, and cook for 5 to 7 minutes. Remove the fillets to a serving plate, and top them with sauce from the pan.

Serves 4

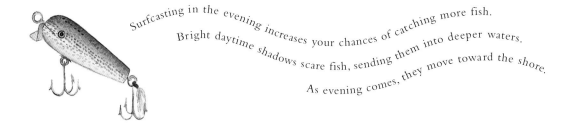

Surfcasting in the evening increases your chances of catching more fish. Bright daytime shadows scare fish, sending them into deeper waters. As evening comes, they move toward the shore.

SALMON AND ASPARAGUS RISOTTO

INGREDIENTS

6 cups chicken broth (not the low-sodium variety)
2 tablespoons olive oil
1 cup chopped onions
1 cup chopped celery
1½ cups arborio rice
½ pound salmon fillet, skinless
20 asparagus spears
3 tablespoons butter, at room temperature
Freshly ground black pepper to taste
¾ cup grated Parmesan cheese

DIRECTIONS

In a medium saucepan, boil the chicken broth and reduce the heat to simmer. While the broth is simmering, heat 1 tablespoon olive oil, onions, and celery in a large saucepan over medium heat until the onions become translucent. Add the rice and sauté for one minute, to coat the rice with oil.

Turn the heat to medium high, and add 1 cup of chicken broth. Bring the mixture to a boil, stirring frequently. Keep the mixture boiling and add the chicken broth, one cup at a time, each time the rice mixture has absorbed the liquid. Stir frequently to prevent the rice from sticking to the bottom of the pot.

Add the asparagus spears to the rice mixture when you have used 3 cups of the chicken broth. Once you have used all the chicken broth (which will take about 25 to 30 minutes), add water to the rice mixture if the rice is still too hard.

In a separate pan, sauté the salmon in 1 tablespoon oil until it is flaky and cooked through, about 7 to 10 minutes. Remove from heat and break the salmon into flakes.

Once the rice has absorbed all the liquid and is just firm, remove the pan from the heat, and stir in the butter, pepper, and Parmesan cheese. Fold the salmon flakes into the risotto.

Serves 4 as a main dish, 6 as an appetizer

Shellfish

It is both relaxing and exciting to dig for clams in the many marshes and tidal areas that line Cape Cod. Reluctant beginners are often the last to leave, staying for hours with cries of "just one more!"

The shore offers a variety of shellfish, which is very simple to prepare. Steamers, quahogs, oysters, mussels, and scallops are some of the most popular shellfish in the area. Steamers are soft-shelled clams that inhabit sandy or muddy areas between low and high tides. Quahogs, also known as Little Necks, cherrystones, or chowders, depending on their size, can be found close to the surface in shallow bays. They were once valued by Native Americans, who made *wampum* from the purple parts of the inner shells. Now a delicacy, oysters were once a staple part of the Pilgrims' diet, providing a vital source of protein. Oysters are identified by the area they come from, and Wellfleet oysters are among the best. The salt and minerals in the water contribute to their taste. Mussels, once frowned upon as peasant food, are now very popular. They cling together in clusters in rocky areas. Scallops, often referred to as bay scallops on the Cape, are found in eel grass beds.

Towns on the Cape are protective of their shellfish supplies due to overharvesting. Before heading off to clam, stop at the local town hall to obtain a permit and find out about the town's laws, quotas, and other restrictions.

Clamming is a good way to observe other types of wildlife. Look for hermit crabs, horseshoe crabs, seagulls, piping plovers, sandpipers, starfish, and moonsnails.

Nauset Marsh, Eastham

clams and lobsters

CLAMMING TIPS

- Take only what you need, and follow local restricions.
- Bacteria grow quickly in dead shellfish. Don't take any shellfish that you find sitting in the sun.
- Wear old sneakers—there are lots of sharp shells and crabs in the marshes!
- Look for clam "signs," small holes or dimples in the sand or mud, which indicate that clams are below.
- Use a small shovel or clamming rake to dig for clams. Dig carefully, especially for steamers, so you don't break the shells or cut your fingers.

HOW TO CLEAN CLAMS:

Scrub clam shells with a stiff brush to remove sand, mud, and barnacles. Then place the clams in a bucket of clear seawater or fresh water to which you've added a cup of salt. Add a cup of cornmeal to the water and allow the clams to sit for 30 minutes. (They will die in unsalted water.) Once the clams have soaked, keep them refrigerated until you are ready to use them.

HOW TO STEAM CLAMS:

Place 1 inch of water in a deep pot and add the clams. Bring the water to a boil, and reduce the heat to simmer. Cover the pot, and allow the clams to steam for 5 to 10 minutes. Discard any clams that don't open. Save the broth, and serve the clams with melted butter, clam broth, and crusty French bread.

HOW TO COOK A LOBSTER:

Make sure that the claws are tightly secured. Boil water in a large stockpot, and plunge the lobster into the boiling water. Allow the lobster to cook for approximately 8 minutes for the first pound and 4 minutes for each subsequent pound. The lobster will be fully cooked when the shell turns bright red. Serve with melted butter and lobster bibs!

HOW TO SHUCK A CLAM OR OYSTER:

Clams and oysters can be quite tricky to open. The basic principle is to sever the muscle that connects the clam meat to the shell. Protect your hands with heavy gloves, or a towel, and use a short, sharp knife. Place the oyster or clam on a flat surface. Insert the tip of the knife between the top and bottom shells. Carefully pry the two shells slightly apart. Holding the blade against the upper shell to avoid cutting the meat, slide the knife back to sever the muscle. Remove the top shell, taking care not to lose any of the liquid. Slide the knife under the clam meat and cut the muscle connecting it to the bottom shell. Serve with lemon juice and cockail sauce.

COCKTAIL SAUCE

INGREDIENTS

1 cup ketchup
2 teaspoons horseradish
1/2 teaspoon chili powder

1 tablespoon fresh lemon juice
Salt and ground black pepper to taste

DIRECTIONS

Stir all the ingredients together in small bowl. Adjust chili powder to taste.

CLAM CHOWDER

INGREDIENTS

8 pounds quahog clams
6 cups cold water
6 tablespoons butter
$^1/_2$ cup diced salt pork
2 medium onions, chopped
6 tablespoons flour

2 cups evaporated milk
10 potatoes, peeled and diced
5 drops hot sauce
1 teaspoon Dijon mustard
1 teaspoon celery seed
1 cup light cream

DIRECTIONS

Thoroughly scrub the clams under running water. Place them in a large stockpot and cover with cold water. Cover the pot, and bring the clams to a boil. Lower the heat to medium, and cook until the clams have opened. Discard any clams that don't open. Remove the clams, reserving the liquid. Then remove the meat from the shells and place it in a bowl. Strain the liquid and return it to the stockpot.

Melt 5 tablespoons of the butter in a saucepan over medium heat. Reduce the heat to low, add the salt pork and onions, and sauté for 5 minutes until the onions are translucent and the salt pork browns. Stir in the flour all at once to make a *roux*. Cook the *roux* over low heat for 3 minutes, stirring continuously. Add 2 cups of the reserved cooking liquid to the *roux*, and whisk it over medium heat until it has thickened. Reduce the heat to low, and add the evaporated milk. Stir until slightly thicker. Then remove the salt pork with a slotted spoon.

Bring the remaining cooking liquid to a boil in the stockpot. Reduce the heat to medium, and add the potatoes, hot sauce, Dijon mustard, and celery seed. Simmer for 10 to 15 minutes, until the potatoes are tender.

Chop the clams and add them, along with the light cream, remaining butter, and *roux*, to the stockpot. Season to taste with salt and pepper.

Serves 8

The word chowder most likely comes from the French word for kettle, *chaudière.*

DADDY'S STUFFED CLAMS (the best!)

Take only what you need, and don't forget your clamming license!

INGREDIENTS

8 pounds quahogs, scrubbed clean
1 cup water
2 tablespoons olive oil
1 large onion, diced
4 garlic cloves, chopped
$^1/_2$ pound linguiça, diced
$^1/_2$ teaspoon pepper
14 ounces preseasoned herb stuffing mix
1–2 lemons, cut in wedges

DIRECTIONS

Boil the water in a large stockpot. Add the quahogs, cover the pot, and steam until the clams open, about 5 to 10 minutes. Discard any clams that don't open. Strain the clam broth, reserving 3 cups. Remove the meat from the opened shells and set it aside to cool. Separate the shells into halves.

Preheat the oven to 375°. Heat the olive oil in a large saucepan. Add the onions, garlic, *linguiça,* and pepper, and sauté over medium heat for 4 to 5 minutes, until the onions become translucent. Over medium heat, add the stuffing mix to the onion mixture and combine. Stir in 2 cups of the reserved clam broth. Finely chop the clams and stir them into the stuffing mixture. If the stuffing appears too dry, add additional clam broth.

Spoon the clam stuffing into the halved clam shells. Bake the clams on a cookie sheet for 10 to 12 minutes, or until the tops are lightly browned. Serve with lemon wedges.

Makes approximately 20 stuffed clams

clambake

THE TRADITION OF A CAPE COD CLAMBAKE *dates back to the Native Americans of the area, who taught the colonists how to cook clams, lobsters, corn, and other goodies in a large pit in the ground. They would dig a large hole, line it with stones, and top it with a hot fire, which would be left to burn for several hours. When the fire burned down, the embers were cleared, and the pit was lined with a thick layer of wet seaweed. Layers of food followed, then more wet seaweed, which would steam the food. A few hours later, the feast would begin!*

CLAMBAKE TIPS

- Always check local laws before building your own bonfire.
- The ingredients in a clambake are cooked with steam, so it is important to keep them moist. Seaweed and a little additional water help!
- If you can find it, use fresh rockweed. This type of seaweed has bubbles in it that crackle and pop while cooking, adding extra liquid and a tasty seaside flavor.
- While steaming, all the flavors intermingle, so feel free to add some *linguiça*, wine, and aromatic seasonings.
- Be prepared with lobster bibs, lobster crackers, washcloths, and extra butter!

STOVE-TOP CLAMBAKE

INGREDIENTS

4 cloves garlic, chopped
$^1/_2$ teaspoon ground thyme
$^1/_2$ teaspoon salt
$^1/_4$ teaspoon ground black pepper
6 ears of corn, shucked
8–10 medium red potatoes

4 live lobsters, about $1^1/_4$ pound each
$1^1/_2$ pounds linguiça
4 pounds steamer clams, cleaned thoroughly
$^1/_2$ pound unsalted butter, melted
3 pounds rockweed (optional)

DIRECTIONS

Pour 1 inch of water into a large 18-quart kettle, and add the garlic, thyme, salt, and pepper. Arrange the corn and potatoes to form the first layer. Cover with a thin layer of rockweed if you are using it. Arrange the lobsters and *linguiça* on top of the potatoes and corn, and then add the clams on top. Add a final layer of rockweed (optional), and cover the pot.

Bring the liquid to a boil over high heat. Reduce the heat to medium and simmer for 30 to 40 minutes, until the clam shells have opened and the lobster is bright red. Remove the contents of the pot, saving the cooking liquid for dipping. Discard any clams that do not open. Arrange the lobster, clams, and vegetables on a large platter, and serve with bowls of melted butter and clam broth.

Serves 4

Many beaches have sandcastle contests in the summer. Build your dream home!

STEAMED MUSSELS

INGREDIENTS

4 pounds mussels
2 tablespoons olive oil
2 cloves garlic, chopped
2 tablespoons chopped shallots
1 teaspoon thyme
Pinch of red pepper flakes
1/2 cup white wine
2 tablespoons lemon juice
1 cup chicken broth
1/4 cup heavy cream
2 tomatoes, peeled and seeded
1/4 cup chopped parsley
2 tablespoons butter
Loaf of crusty French bread

DIRECTIONS

Rinse the mussels thoroughly and scrub them with a vegetable brush.

Heat the olive oil in a large stockpot over medium heat. Add the garlic, shallots, thyme, and pepper flakes and sauté for 2 to 3 minutes. Add the white wine, lemon juice, chicken broth, heavy cream, and mussels. Cover the pot and simmer over medium heat for 5 to 7 minutes, until the mussels open. Add the tomatoes, parsley, and butter, cover the pot, and continue to simmer for another minute. Serve in the broth with French bread.

Serves 4

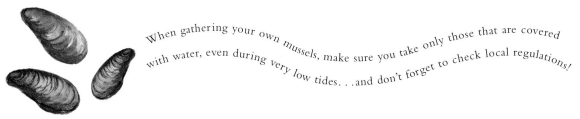

When gathering your own mussels, make sure you take only those that are covered with water, even during very low tides. . .and don't forget to check local regulations!

Linguini with Clam Sauce

INGREDIENTS

32 Little Neck clams
4 tablespoons olive oil
2 tablespoons butter
4 cloves garlic, chopped
$^1/_4$ teaspoon dried sweet basil
$^1/_4$ teaspoon dried oregano
$^1/_4$ teaspoon salt
$^1/_4$ teaspoon black pepper
$^1/_2$ cup white wine
4 tablespoons chopped fresh parsley
Linguini to serve 4
Parmesan cheese

DIRECTIONS

Scrub the clams. Heat the olive oil and butter in a large saucepan over low heat. Add the garlic, basil, oregano, salt, and pepper. Sauté over low heat for 3 minutes. Add the wine and whole clams, cover, and simmer until the clams open, approximately 5 to 7 minutes. Discard any clams that have not opened. Remove half the clams from the pot.

Remove the meat from the shells and chop it into small pieces. Add the chopped clams to the sauce, along with the parsley. Continue to simmer for 5 more minutes.

Cook the linguini according to the package directions. Divide it into shallow bowls and top with the sauce. Arrange the remaining whole clams evenly among the plates. Serve with Parmesan cheese and fresh French bread.

Serves 4

Clam rings protect quahogs from being overharvested. If the clam doesn't fit through the ring, put it back. Clams 2-2$^1/_4$" are called Little Necks, 2$^1/_4$"-3" are cherrystones, and 3" and up are "chowders."

FETTUCINE WITH SCALLOPS AND SHRIMP

INGREDIENTS

4 tablespoons olive oil
1 medium onion, chopped
2 garlic cloves, chopped
6 ounces mushrooms, thinly sliced
1 cup white wine
2 chicken bouillon cubes
2 cups heavy cream
12 large shrimp, peeled and deveined

³/₄ pounds bay scallops
4 Italian plum tomatoes, peeled, seeded, and chopped
¹/₄ cup grated Parmesan cheese
¹/₃ cup chopped fresh parsley
Salt and pepper to taste
1 pound fettucine
Fresh chopped parsley for garnish

DIRECTIONS

In a large saucepan, sauté the onions, garlic, and mushrooms in the olive oil over medium heat for 3 to 5 minutes, until the onions become translucent. Whisk in the wine, add the bouillon cubes, and bring to a boil. Lower the heat to simmer and cook, uncovered, until the liquid is reduced by half, about 5 to 7 minutes.

Add the heavy cream, and continue to simmer on low heat until the sauce is slightly thickened. Add the shrimp, scallops, and tomatoes and simmer for 3 minutes. Stir in the Parmesan cheese and parsley and cook 1 minute longer.

Cook the fettucine according to the package directions. Top with the scallop and shrimp sauce and garnish with parsley. Serve with additional Parmesan cheese.

Serves 4

While sailing and fishing around Cape Cod in 1602, Bartholomew Gosnold noticed that his men were catching vast numbers of cod, so he labeled the area Cape Cod on his map.

LOBSTER ROLL

Many people are purists when it comes to their lobster rolls, preferring nothing but lobster meat, melted butter, and salt. The more adventurous might like to add one of the optional ingredients we've listed below.

INGREDIENTS

1 pound cooked lobster meat, chopped
$^1/_2$ cup finely chopped celery
1 tablespoon lemon juice
$^1/_3$ cup mayonnaise, approximate
Salt
Freshly ground pepper
4 frankfurter rolls
Softened butter

OPTIONAL INGREDIENTS

Pinch of curry powder
1 tablespoon capers
3 tablespoons grated onion

Pinch of cayenne pepper powder
1 tablespoon fresh dill
Lettuce, shredded

DIRECTIONS

Combine the lobster meat, celery, and lemon juice. Mix slightly, and then add just enough mayonnaise to bind the mixture, and stir well. Add salt and pepper to taste and mix well.

Split the rolls if necessary. Butter them on both sides, and slowly toast them over low heat in a large frying pan until both sides are lightly browned. Scoop the lobster salad onto the toasted rolls. Keep cool until ready to serve.

Serves 4

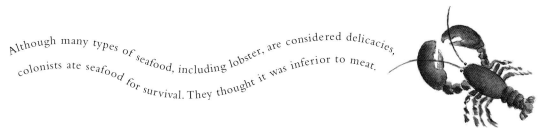

Although many types of seafood, including lobster, are considered delicacies, colonists ate seafood for survival. They thought it was inferior to meat.

Desserts

Original Cape Cod desserts, like many of the dishes made by the Pilgrims, tended to be hearty and filling. Desserts were often made with local fruits and sweetened with maple sugar or molasses. Many had biscuit toppings that were either baked or steamed. The names given to these desserts reflect their filling nature: pandowdy,

grunt, slump, cobbler, and fool. Fruits and berries were preserved into jellies and jams to last during long winter months.

The Cape has many delightful old-fashioned candy stores featuring a selection of fudge and taffy. Saltwater taffy, a popular treat, traces its origins to the boardwalks of Atlantic City, New Jersey. Some candy stores have machines that pull the taffy, and it's fun to watch the process. And the many ice cream shops lining Routes 6 and 6A are tempting stops en route to almost any destination!

As the sun sets, a favorite pasttime on the Cape is telling stories about local legends around the campfire. The Native Americans would tell the tale of Maushop, the giant who created Cape Cod. In later years, tales of the mooncussers—scoundrels who would lure ships to shallow waters—and speculation over the ill-fated romance of Captain "Black Sam" Bellamy and Goody Hallett have captured listeners of all ages.

Sprinkles are called "Jimmies" on Cape Cod!

Campgrounds, Oak Bluffs

APPLE-BLUEBERRY PANDOWDY

INGREDIENTS

5 cups peeled, sliced apples
1/2 pint (1 cup) blueberries
3 tablespoons maple syrup
1/4 cup brown sugar
1 teaspoon cinnamon
1 cup flour
1/4 cup sugar

2 teaspoons baking powder
1/2 teaspoon salt
1/2 cup milk
1 egg
1/4 cup butter, melted
1 teaspoon vanilla

DIRECTIONS

Preheat the oven to 350°. Grease a shallow 8 x 8-inch baking dish.

In a medium bowl, mix the apples and blueberries with the maple syrup, brown sugar, and cinnamon. Place the mixture in the prepared baking dish, cover it with aluminum foil, and bake for 30 minutes.

Meanwhile, whisk together the flour, sugar, baking powder, and salt. Stir in the milk, egg, melted butter, and vanilla. Pour the mixture over the baked apples and blueberries, and return the pan to the oven and bake for 30 minutes, or until a toothpick inserted in the center comes out clean. Serve with whipped cream or ice cream.

Serves 6

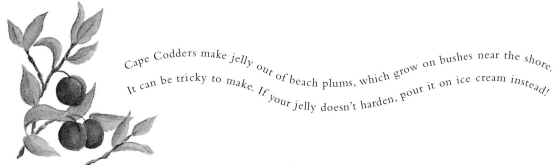

Cape Codders make jelly out of beach plums, which grow on bushes near the shore. It can be tricky to make. If your jelly doesn't harden, pour it on ice cream instead!

YANKEE DOODLE SHORTCAKE

INGREDIENTS

Sauce & Topping:

1 ½ cups blueberries
1 ½ cups strawberries, cut into pieces
1 teaspoon water

3 tablespoons sugar
1 cup heavy cream

Shortcake:

1 ¾ cups flour
¼ cup sugar
2 teaspoons baking powder
½ teaspoon baking soda

6 tablespoons butter, chilled, cut into small pieces
½ cup buttermilk
1 egg

DIRECTIONS

Sauce & Topping:

Place ½ cup blueberries and ½ cup strawberries in a bowl, sprinkle with water and 1 tablespoon sugar, and mash with a fork to release the juice.

With an electric mixer, whip the cream in a chilled bowl until it forms semi-stiff peaks. Add 2 tablespoons sugar. Mix the remaining berries into the whipped cream.

Shortcake:

Preheat the oven to 400°. Generously grease a cookie sheet.

Combine the flour, sugar, baking powder, and baking soda in a bowl. Add the pieces of chilled butter and mix until crumbly, working through with your fingers. Mix in the buttermilk and egg with a fork until the dough is evenly moistened.

Flour your hands and knead the dough on a lightly floured surface so that it holds together. Pat the dough until it is about ¾ inch thick. Cut it into circles with a 2 ½-inch round cookie cutter. Arrange the shortcake biscuits on a cookie sheet. Bake for 8 to 10 minutes, until they are light golden brown on top.

Pour the mashed berry sauce over the biscuits and spoon on the whipped cream topping.

Serves 6

DAFFODIL CAKE

INGREDIENTS

White Batter:

1 cup cake flour
1¹/₂ cups sugar
2 tablespoons confectioner's sugar
10–12 egg whites (1³/₄ cups)
1¹/₂ teaspoons cream of tartar
¹/₄ teaspoon salt
1¹/₂ teaspoons vanilla
¹/₂ teaspoon lemon extract

Yellow Batter:

6 egg yolks
2 tablespoons grated lemon peel
1 tablespoon sugar
1 tablespoon confectioner's sugar

Glaze:

1¹/₄ cups confectioner's sugar
1 tablespoon lemon juice
3 tablespoons half and half
1 tablespoon melted butter

DIRECTIONS

Preheat the oven to 375°. Sift the cake flour, ³/₄ cup sugar, and confectioner's sugar together twice.

In a large mixing bowl, beat the egg whites, cream of tartar, and salt on high speed until foamy. Continue to beat on high speed while slowly adding the remaining ³/₄ cup sugar, until the meringue holds stiff peaks when you lift up the beaters. Gently fold in the vanilla and lemon extract.

In a smaller mixing bowl, begin making the yellow batter. Beat the egg yolks, grated lemon peel, sugar and confectioner's sugar until the mixture thickens and becomes light yellow.

Slowly and gently fold the flour mixture into the meringue. Pour one-third of this white batter into a separate bowl, and gently fold in the yellow batter. Pour the batters into an ungreased tube pan, alternating layers of white and yellow batter. Using a knife, swirl the batters. Bake for 35 to 40 minutes, until the top of the cake is golden brown and springs back when you touch it lightly.

Invert the cake pan on a funnel until it is completely cool. While it is cooling, make the glaze by mixing all the ingredients until smooth. Remove the cooled cake from the pan, glaze it, and sprinkle it with confectioner's sugar.

Serves 8-10

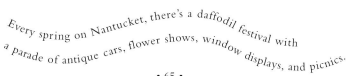

Every spring on Nantucket, there's a daffodil festival with a parade of antique cars, flower shows, window displays, and picnics.

A Cape Cod Legend

The Story of Captain "Black Sam" Bellamy and Goody Hallett

As THE CAMPFIRES GLOW and the stars shine bright on the shores of the Cape, no doubt someone will begin to tell you the story of Captain Black Sam Bellamy and his beloved, Goody Hallett. There are many versions of the tale, and, while some of them are fact and some fiction, old timers will tell you that one thing is true: If you find yourself walking through the dunes of Wellfleet late at night, you're sure to experience a few odd things ... or perhaps you already have.

It all started way back in 1715 when Sam Bellamy, a young English sailor, came to the colonies to seek his fortune. While spending a summer on Cape Cod, Bellamy met Maria "Goody" Hallett, a beautiful young girl from Eastham. They fell in love and he wanted desperately to marry her, yet he feared that her father would doubt his intentions because he was not a wealthy man. Upon hearing of a ferocious hurricane in the Bahamas that shipwrecked many vessels laden with riches from Spain, Bellamy convinced a wealthy merchant named Palgrave Williams to outfit a ship that he could use to search for the gold, and he set off for the islands. He asked Goody to wait for him, and promised they would marry upon his return.

Uncovering the lost treasure was not to be Bellamy's fortune. Instead, he and his band of buccaneers began looting ships on the high seas. He could not return to the Cape without the riches he felt he needed to win Goody, and he became an outlaw. A dashing fellow with long black hair tied in a black bow, he became known as Captain Black Sam Bellamy, notorious captain of a legendary pirate crew, renowned for his boldness and generosity to his victims. He and his prosperous fleet looted over 50 ships in the Caribbean in the course of several years.

The pirates lived by their own laws and formed their own social structure. Many of Bellamy's men were captured from African slave ships. He gave them a choice. They could join his crew or continue to their destinations to be sold into slavery.

Although his riches continued to grow, he missed Goody and never forgot his promise to her. After several successful years of piracy, he decided to set sail back to Eastham in a treasure-laden boat, the *Whydah*, a slave ship that he had captured off the coast of Cuba. He had the boat outfitted with a beautiful bell, on which was inscribed "Whydah Gally 1716." He intended to ring the bell as he approached the shores of Eastham to let Goody know that he was returning to her, and that they could be married.

Goody, who had heard rumors that Bellamy was returning to her, went to the shores night after night with a lantern to light the way for him. One stormy evening in April 1717, as she began to walk the shores, she heard the sound of the bell he had made for her. Seeing her lantern on the shore, Bellamy began to sail toward her. However, the ship was caught in the terrible gale and ran aground on the treacherous sandbars off the shores of Wellfleet. Goody, carrying her lantern, ran across the sandbars to try to help save him.

Bellamy and most of his crew were lost in the terrible wreck, and poor Goody became ill with grief. Some say she continues to return to the dunes each night, calling to Bellamy in hopes that he is still trying to reach her. When you hear the sound of a bell ringing offshore, or see a light wavering in the dunes, you may stop and wonder about the tale of Bellamy and Goody.

While some of this story is fact, much of it is fiction. The true story is beginning to be unraveled at the Expedition Whydah Sea Lab & Learning Center on MacMillan Wharf in Provincetown, which now houses the treasures found from the shipwreck of the Whydah.

S'MORES

No campfire is complete without the perfect storytelling snack . . . s'mores. Here's what you'll need for yours:

INGREDIENTS

Lots of friends
A good storyteller
A bag or two of marshmallows
Graham crackers
Chocolate bars
Long, pointy sticks

DIRECTIONS

Put a couple of marshmallows on the end of a stick. Put the stick into the fire until the marshmallows are toasty brown. Place a piece of the chocolate bar on a graham cracker, top with the roasted marshmallows and another graham cracker. Enjoy!

CRANBERRY FUDGE

INGREDIENTS

6 ounces dried cranberries
1/2 cup light corn syrup
2 cups semisweet chocolate chips
1/2 cup confectioner's sugar
1/4 cup plus 1 tablespoon evaporated milk
1 teaspoon vanilla
1/2 cup white chocolate chips

DIRECTIONS

Grease the bottom and sides of an 8 x 8-inch pan.

In a 3-quart saucepan, bring the cranberries and corn syrup to a boil. Boil on high for 5 minutes, stirring occasionally, until the liquid has been reduced. Remove from the heat.

Stir in the semisweet chocolate chips, confectioner's sugar, 1/4 cup evaporated milk, and vanilla, until the mixture thickens and becomes glossy. Spread the mixture evenly in the prepared pan.

Heat the white chocolate and 1 tablespoon evaporated milk in a small saucepan, stirring frequently until melted. Drizzle over the chocolate fudge. Cover, and chill until firm.

PENUCHE FUDGE

INGREDIENTS

4 cups brown sugar
1 cup heavy cream
2 tablespoons butter
1 teaspoon evaporated milk or heavy cream
1 teaspoon vanilla
2 cups chopped walnuts

DIRECTIONS

Grease the bottom and sides of an 8 x 8-inch pan.

In a 3-quart saucepan, combine the brown sugar, heavy cream, and butter. Bring to a rapid, rolling boil for 7 to 10 minutes. Use caution, as the mixture will become frothy and very hot. Continue to boil until a small amount forms a soft, round ball when dropped in cold water.

Remove from the heat, add 1 teaspoon evaporated milk (or heavy cream) and vanilla. Beat rapidly with a wooden spoon for about 2 minutes, until the mixture loses its glossiness. Add nuts, and spread into the prepared pan. Chill before cutting.

drinks

ATLANTIC FLOAT

INGREDIENTS

32 ounces ginger ale
2 cups cranberry juice
4 scoops lime sherbet
Lime wedges for garnish

DIRECTIONS

Pour 8 ounces of ginger ale and ½ cup of cranberry juice into each of four 12-ounce glasses. Add a scoop of lime sherbet, and garnish with a lime wedge.

Serves 4

SUMMER SMOOTHIE

INGREDIENTS

1 cup frozen strawberries
½ cup fresh or frozen cranberries
3 cups orange juice
1 cup cranberry juice
8 ounces raspberry yogurt
2 scoops vanilla frozen yogurt or ice cream

DIRECTIONS

Put all the ingredients in a blender and blend until smooth. Serve immediately in tall glasses.

Serves 2

CRAN-RASPBERRY ICED TEA

INGREDIENTS

6 ounces frozen cranberry juice
2 cups orange juice
¼ cup sugar
2 quarts unsweetened iced tea
Lemon slices for garnish

DIRECTIONS

In a large pitcher, combine the cranberry juice, orange juice, and sugar until they are well mixed and the sugar dissolves. Pour in the iced tea. Serve in ice-filled glasses garnished with lemon slices.

Serves 4

CAPE CODDER

INGREDIENTS

1½ ounces vodka
4 ounces cranberry juice
1 wedge lime

DIRECTIONS

Pour the vodka and cranberry juice over ice in a tall glass. Stir well, and add a wedge of lime.

Makes 1 drink

SEABREEZE

INGREDIENTS

1½ ounces vodka
4 ounces cranberry juice
1 ounce grapefruit juice

DIRECTIONS

Pour the vodka, cranberry juice, and grapefruit juice over ice in a tall glass. Stir well.

Makes 1 drink

INDEX *of recipes and crafts*

Acorn squash, and pear, baked, 23
Anadama bread, 18
Apple-blueberry pandowdy, 62
Asian marinade, 43
Atlantic float, 70

Baked beans, maple, 13
Baked haddock with garlic
    breadcrumbs, 44
Baked pear and acorn squash, 23
Bass, sautéed with prosciutto, 46
Bayberry candles, 24-25
Boston brown bread, 19
Bread, anadama, 18; Boston brown,
    19; Portuguese sweet, 29

Cape Codder, 71
Chutney, cranberry-pear, 39
Clambake, stove-top, 55
Clambake, tips, 54
Clam chowder, 52; Portuguese, 30
Clam sauce, linguini with, 57
Clams, stuffed, 53
Cocktail sauce, 51
Corn muffins, 12
Cornhusk dolls, 14-15
Cranberry fudge, 69
Cranberry sauce, 39
Cranberry-apple-pear sauce, 38
Cranberry-chocolate nut squares, 37
Cranberry-nut muffins, 36
Cranberry-pear chutney, 39
Cran-raspberry iced tea, 71
Cran-raspberry vinaigrette, 38

Daddy's stuffed clams, 53
Daffodil cake, 65

Fettucine, with scallops and
    shrimp, 58
Flan, Portuguese, 31
Fudge, cranberry, 69; penuche, 69

Garlic-dill marinade, 42

Haddock, baked, with
    garlic breadcrumbs, 44
Hash, red flannel, 20

Indian pudding, 21

Journey pancakes, 12

Kale soup, Provincetown, 28

Linguini with clam sauce, 57
Lobster roll, 59

Maple baked beans, 13
Marinade, Asian, 43; garlic-dill, 42;
    orange-basil, 42; rosemary-thyme,
    43; white wine, 43; *vinho d'alhos,* 43
Muffins, corn, 12; cranberry-nut, 36
Mussels, steamed, 56

New England boiled dinner, 20

Orange-basil marinade, 42

Pancakes, journey, 12
Pear, and acorn squash, baked, 23
Penuche fudge, 69
Portuguese clam chowder, 30
Portuguese flan, 31
Portuguese sweet bread, 29
Provincetown kale soup, 28

Red flannel hash, 20
Risotto, salmon and asparagus, 47
Rosemary-thyme marinade, 43

Salmon and asparagus risotto, 47
Sauce, cocktail, 51; cranberry, 39;
    cranberry-apple-pear, 38
Sautéed bass with prosciutto, 46
Scallops, with fettucine and
    shrimp, 58
Seabreeze, 71

Shortcake, Yankee Doodle, 63
Shrimp, with fettucine and
    scallops, 58
Smoothie, summer, 70
S'mores, 68
Steamed mussels, 56
Stew, Three Sisters, 11
Stove-top clambake, 55
Stuffed clams, 53
Succotash, 13
Summer smoothie, 70
Sweet bread, Portuguese, 29
Swordfish kebabs, 45

Tea, cran-raspberry iced, 71
Three Sisters garden, 10
Three Sisters stew, 11
Turkey cutlets, 22

Vinaigrette, cran-raspberry, 38
Vinho d'alhos, 43

White wine marinade, 43
Wild rice, 23

Yankee Doodle shortcake, 63

*Once Cape Cod
sand gets into your
shoes, you will
always return!*